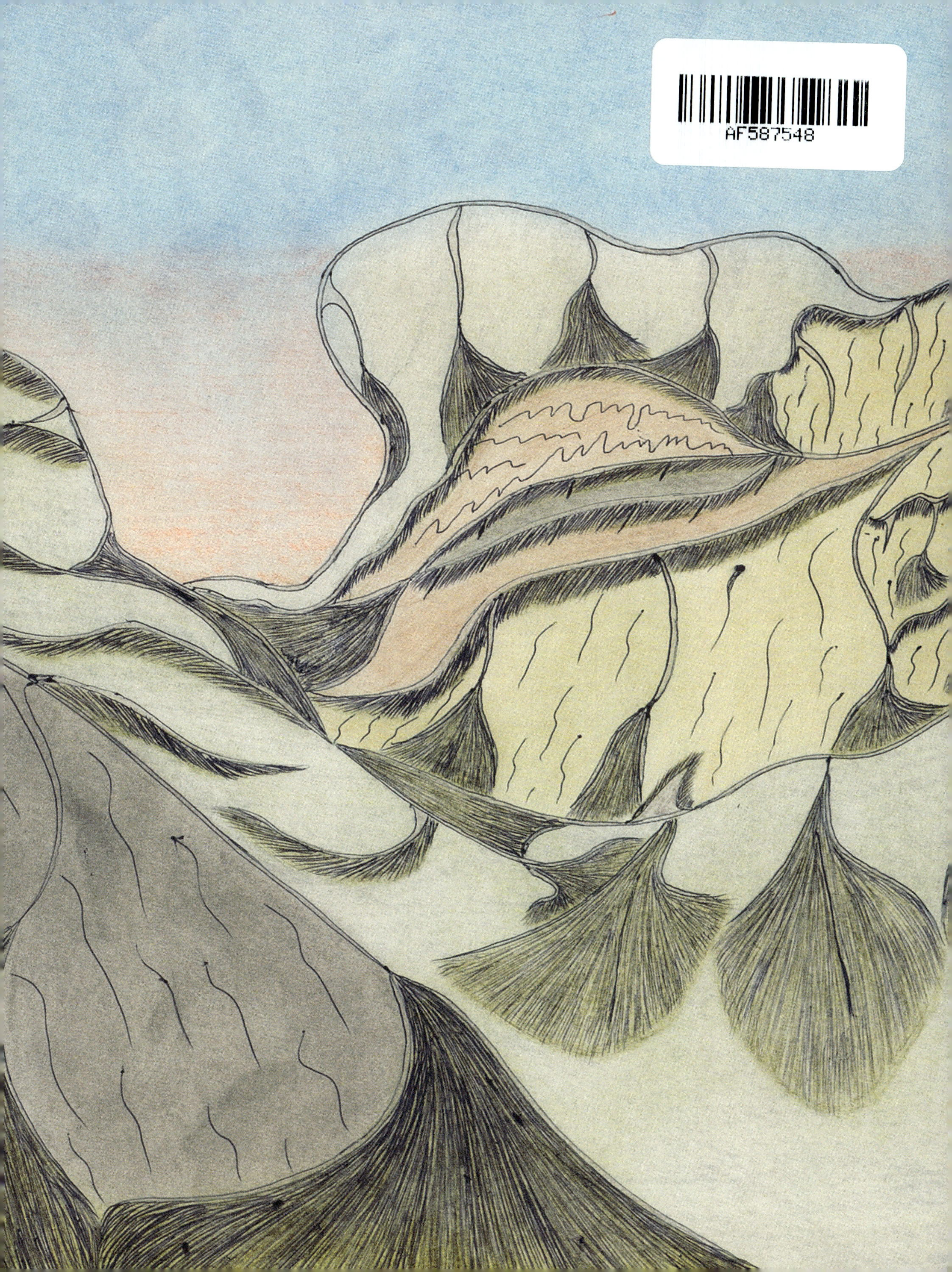

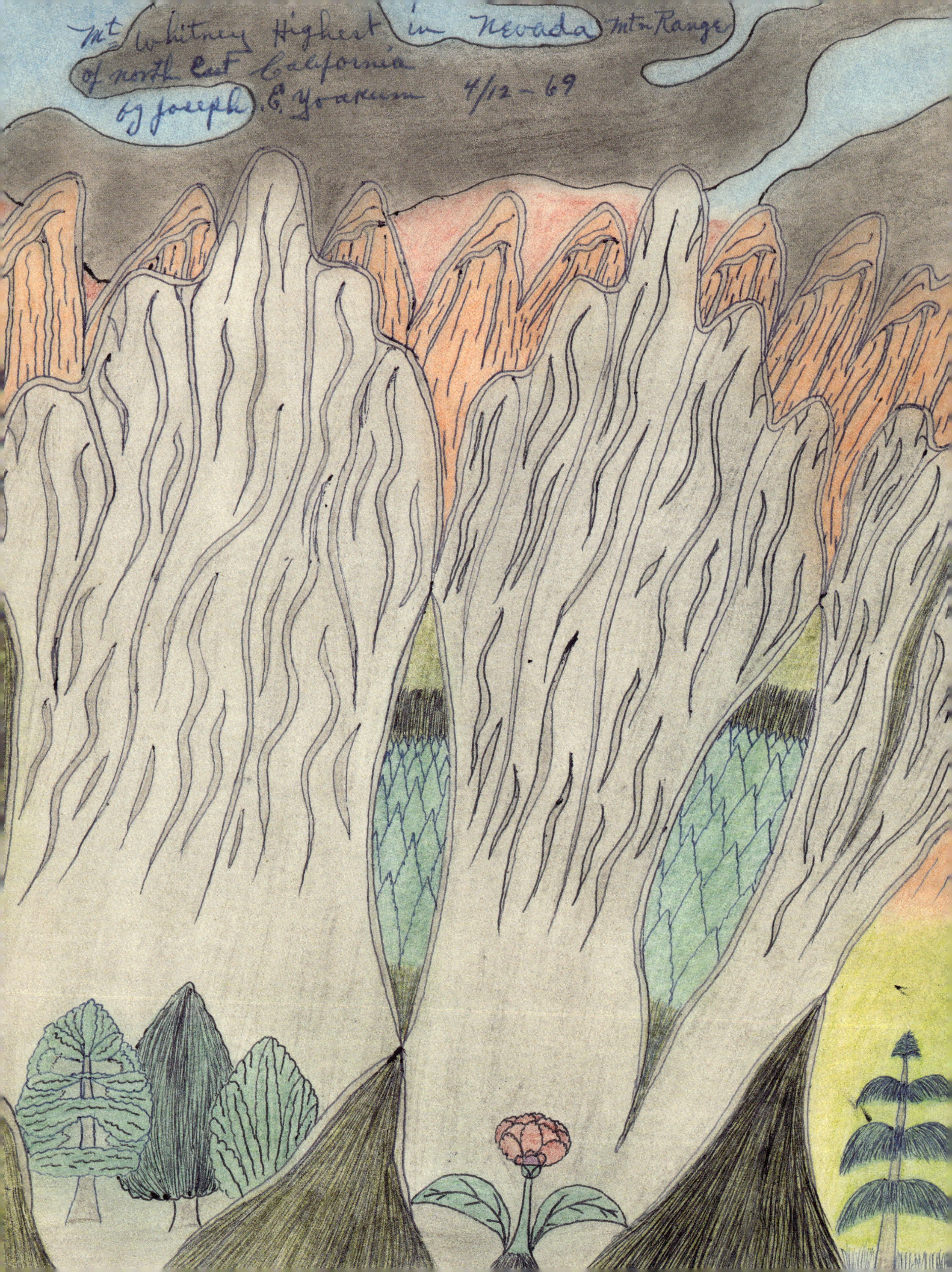
Mt Whitney Highest in Nevada Mtn Range
of north East California
by joseph. E. Yoakum 4/12-69

Mt Cavalary {near Jerusalam and Bethélam} se palestine asia

by joseph E. Yoakum

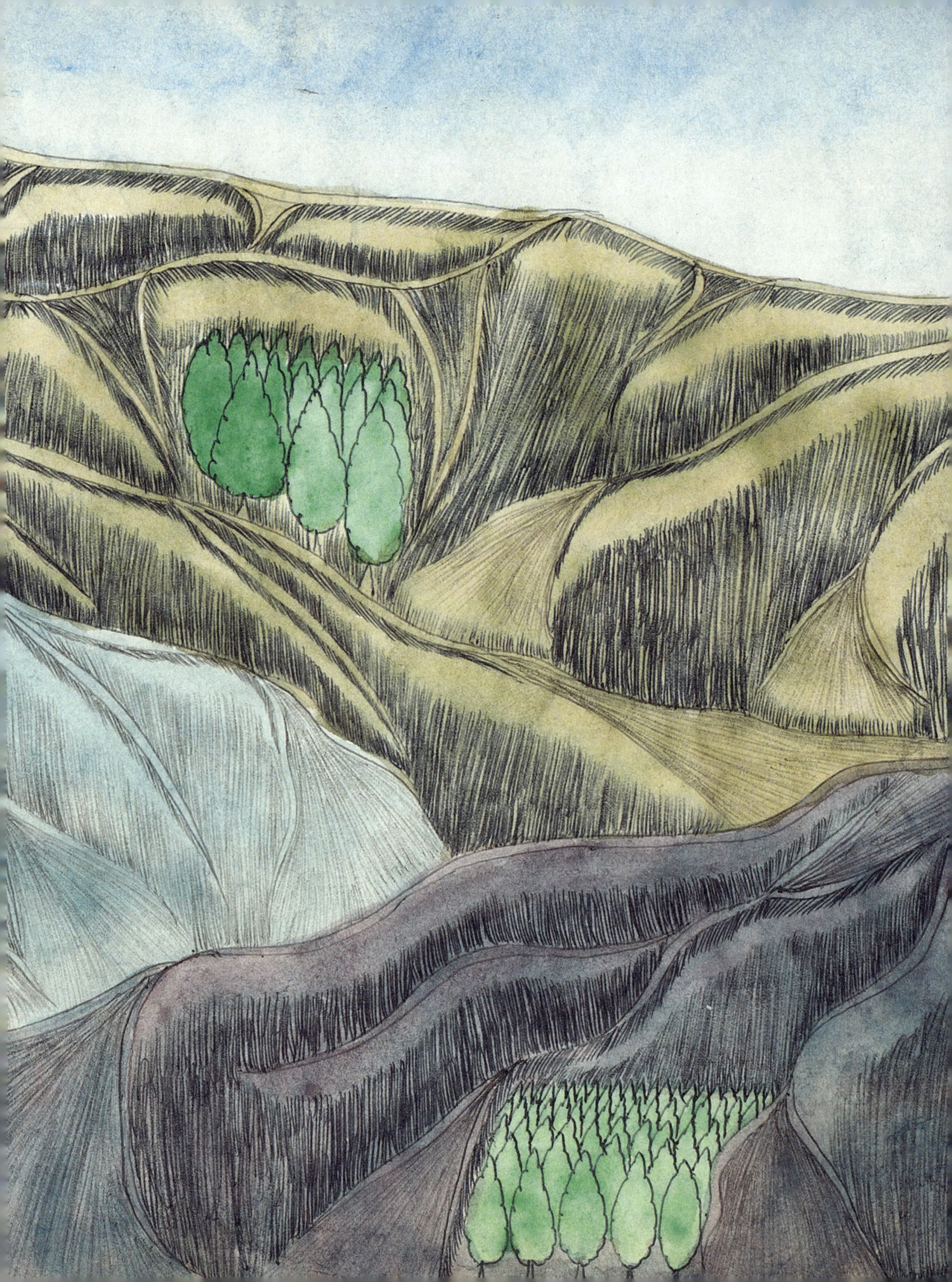

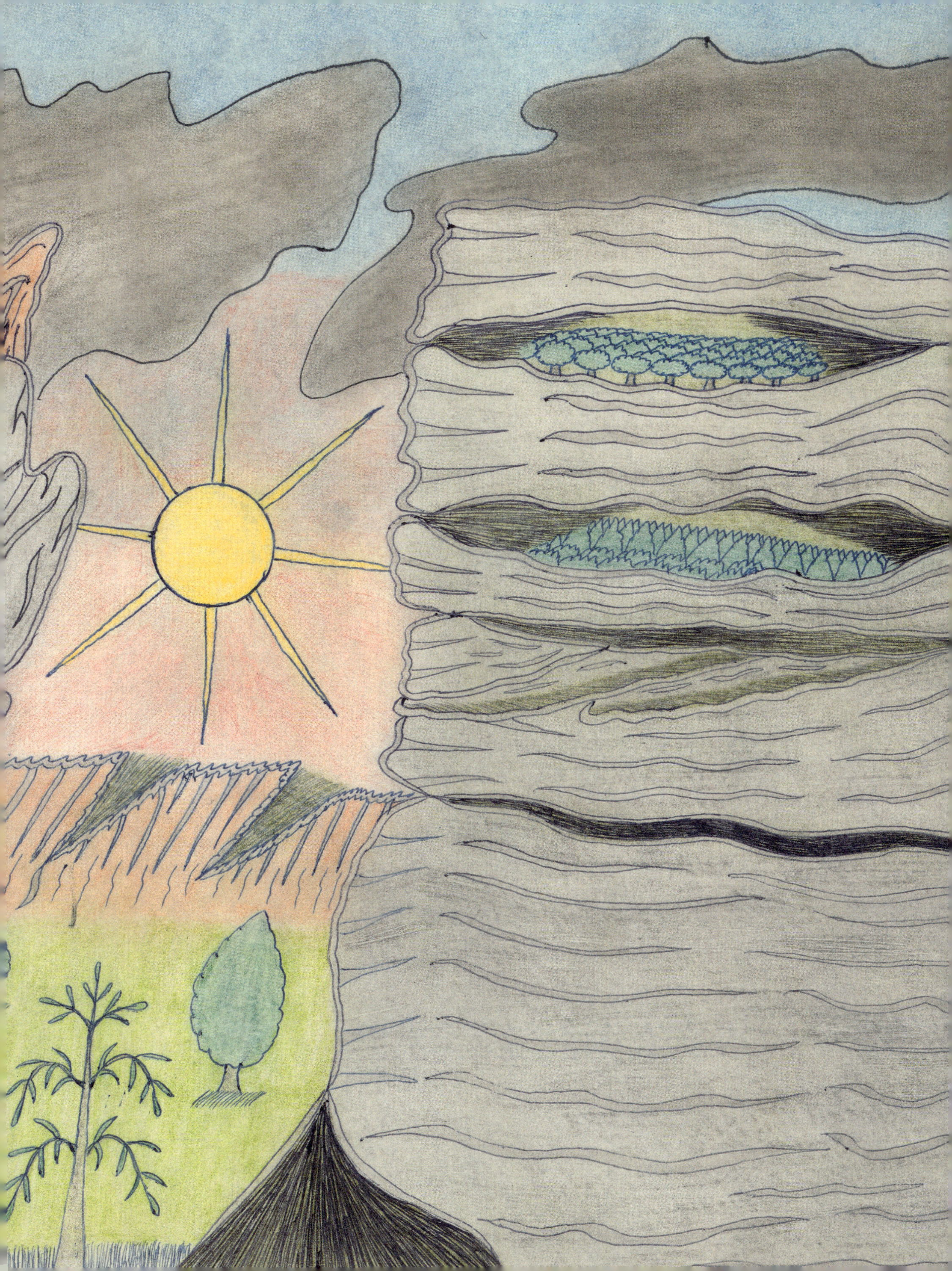

Mt Victoria of Arakan Range
near Village Maungdew Burma E asia
by Joseph E. Yoakum 4/3-69

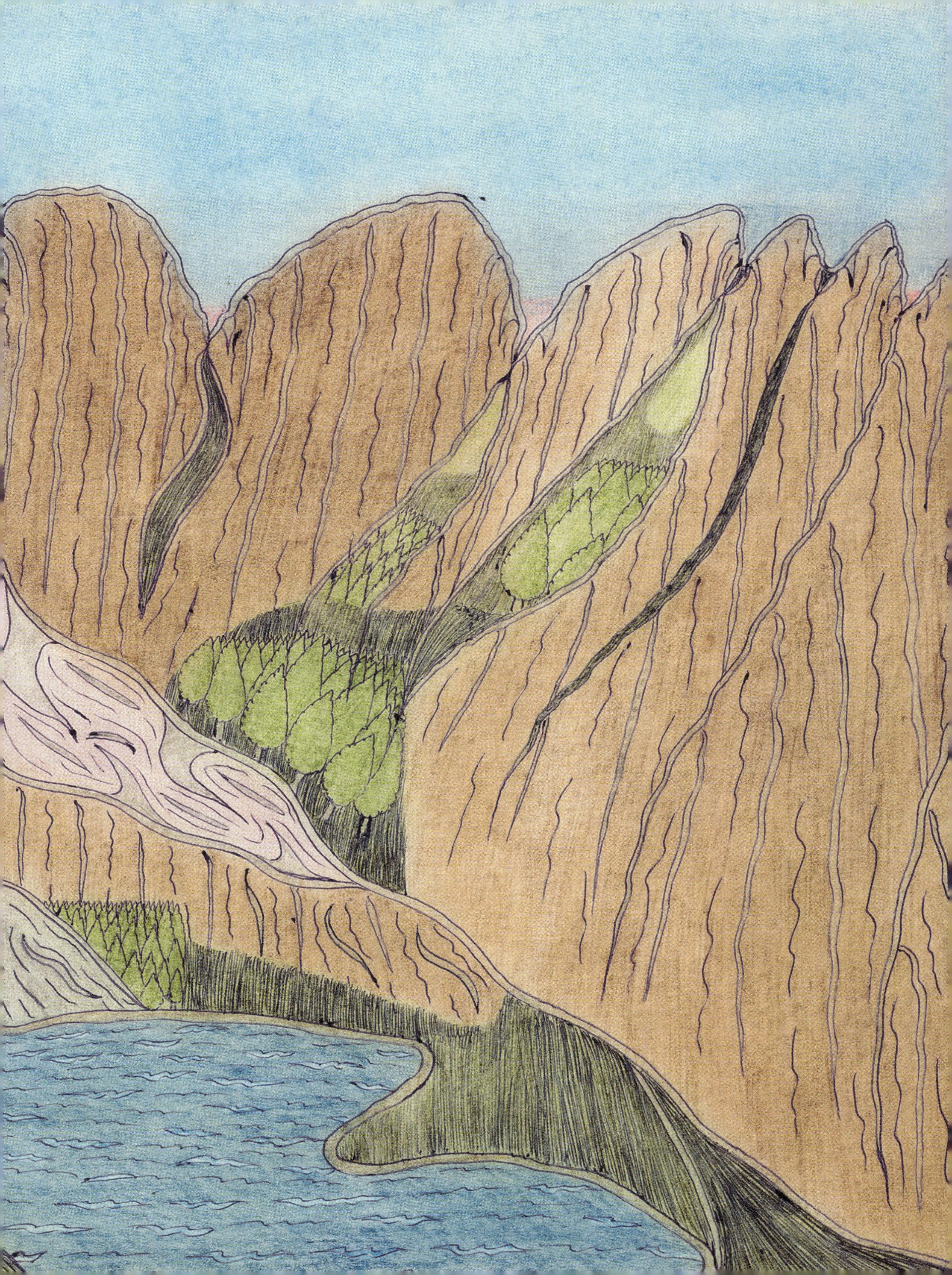

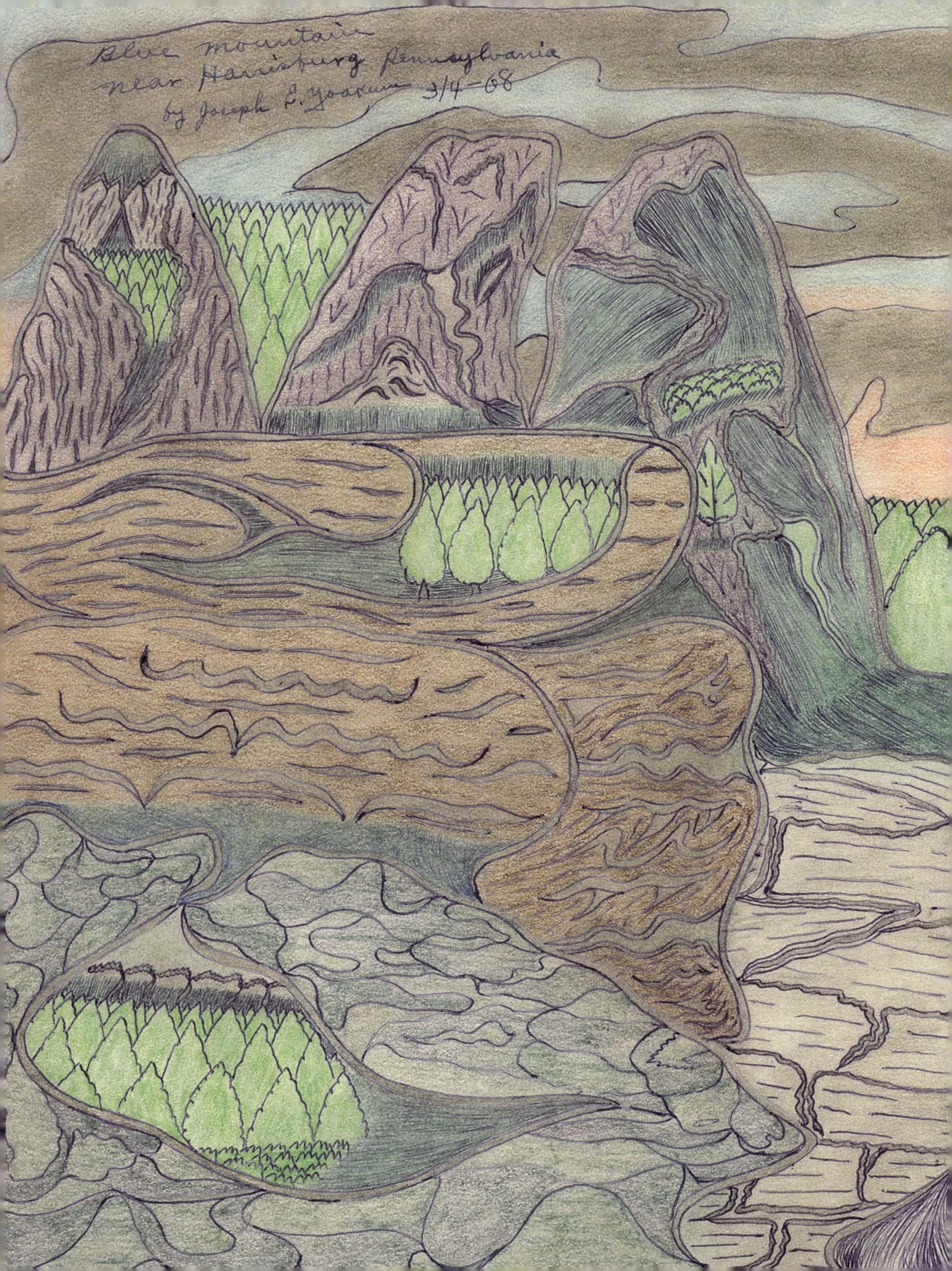
Blue mountain
near Harrisburg pennsylvania
by Joseph E. Yoakum 3/4-68

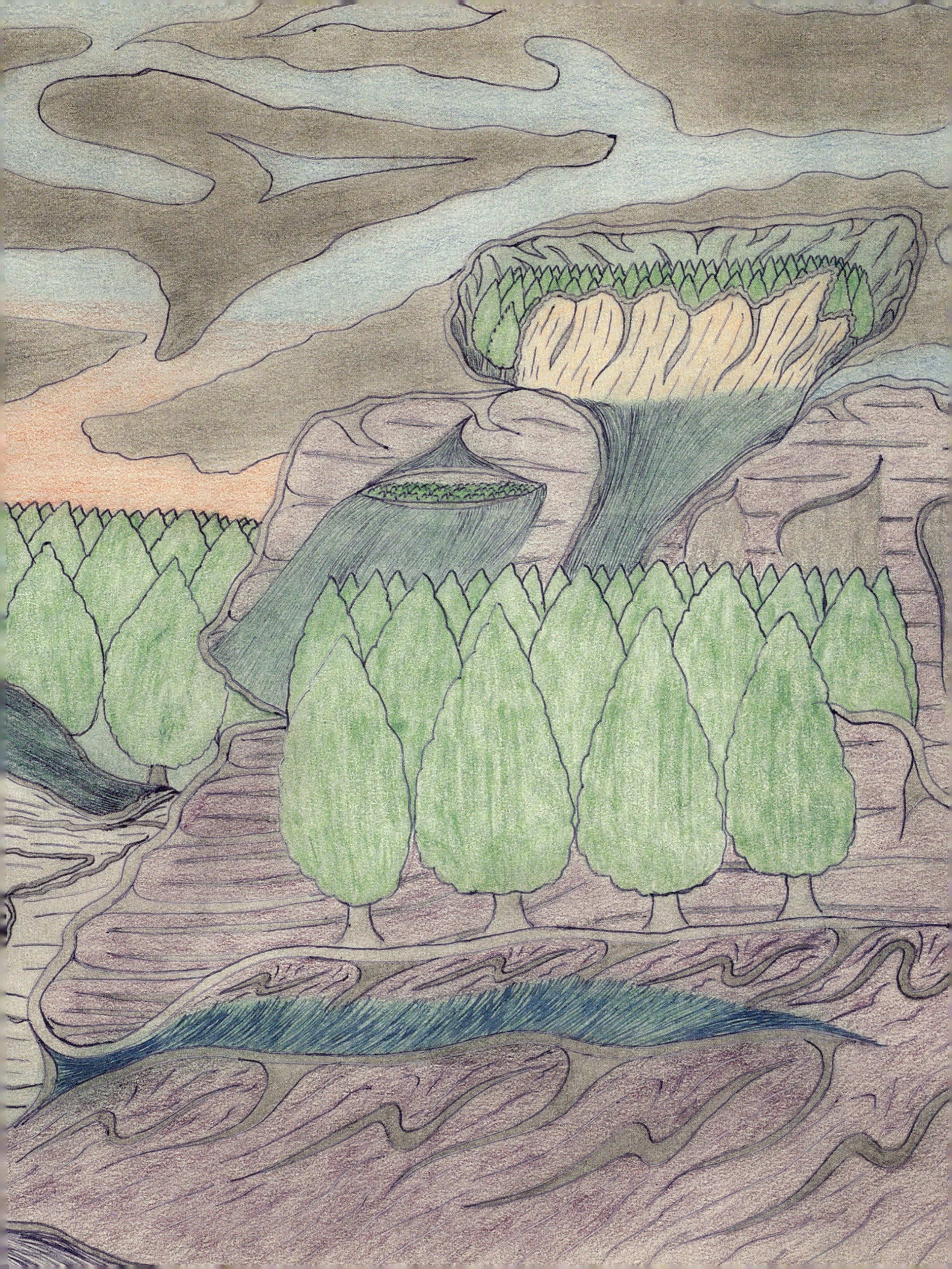

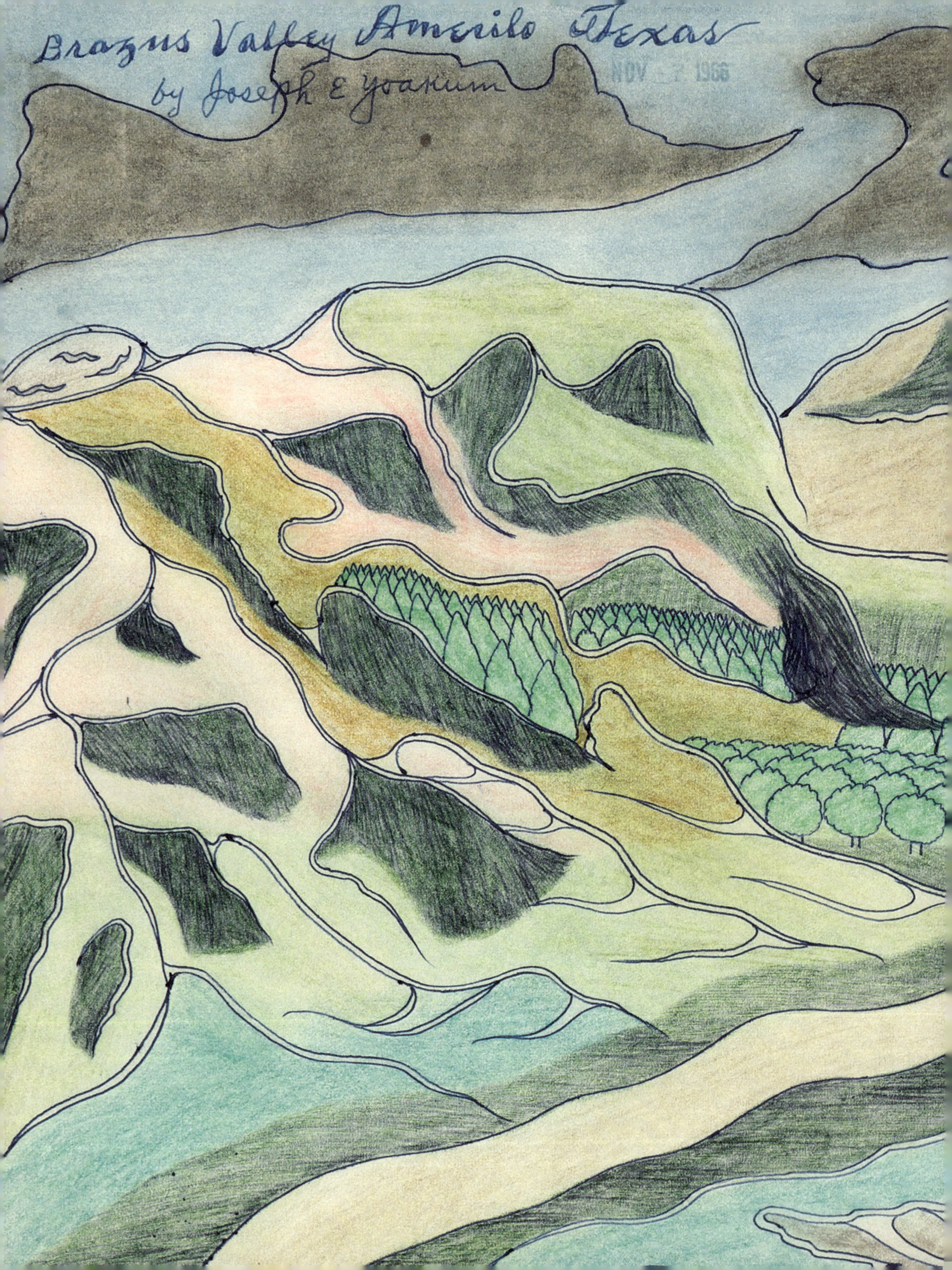
Brazus Valley Amerilo Texas
by Joseph E Yoakum
NOV 1966

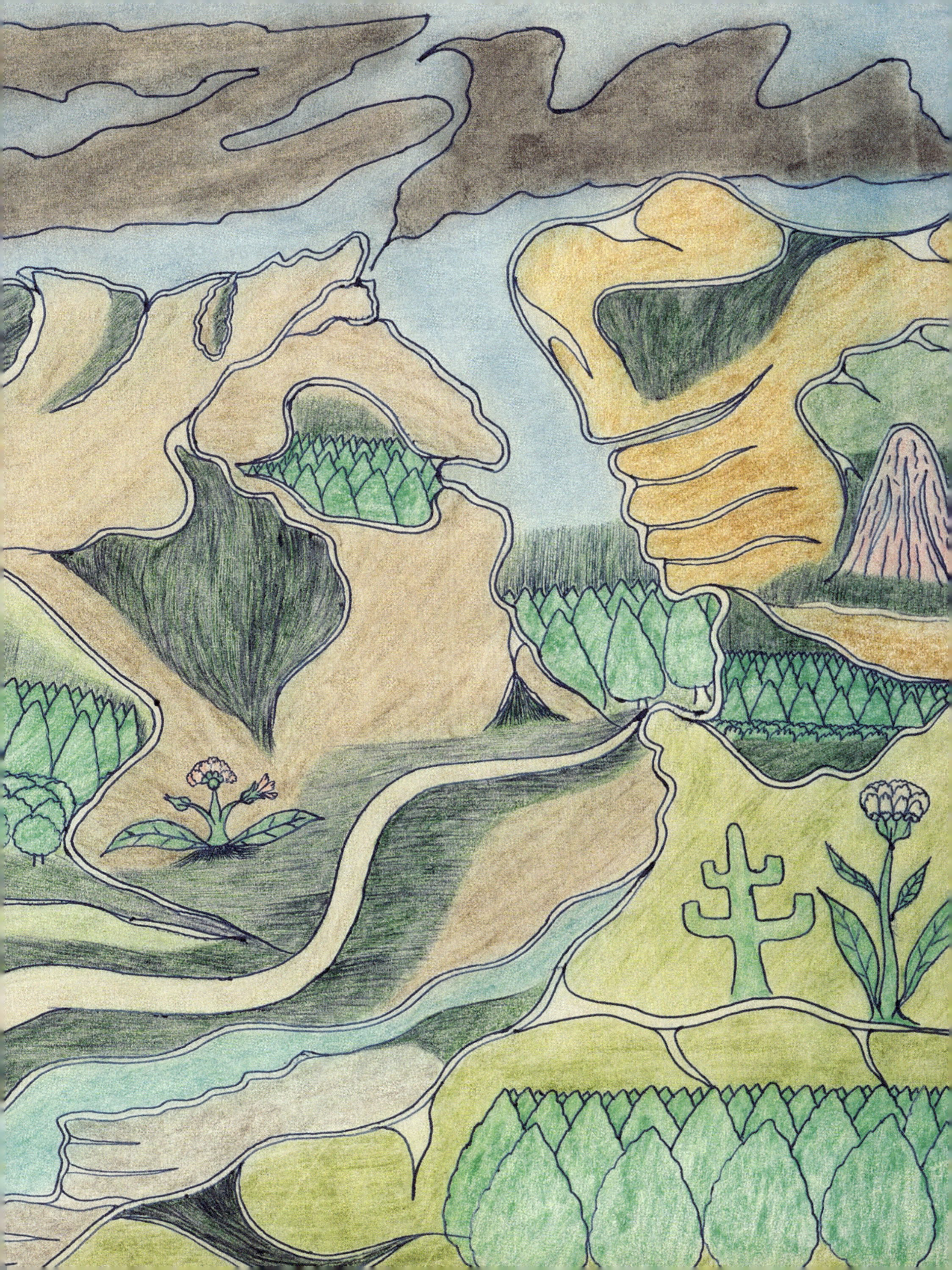

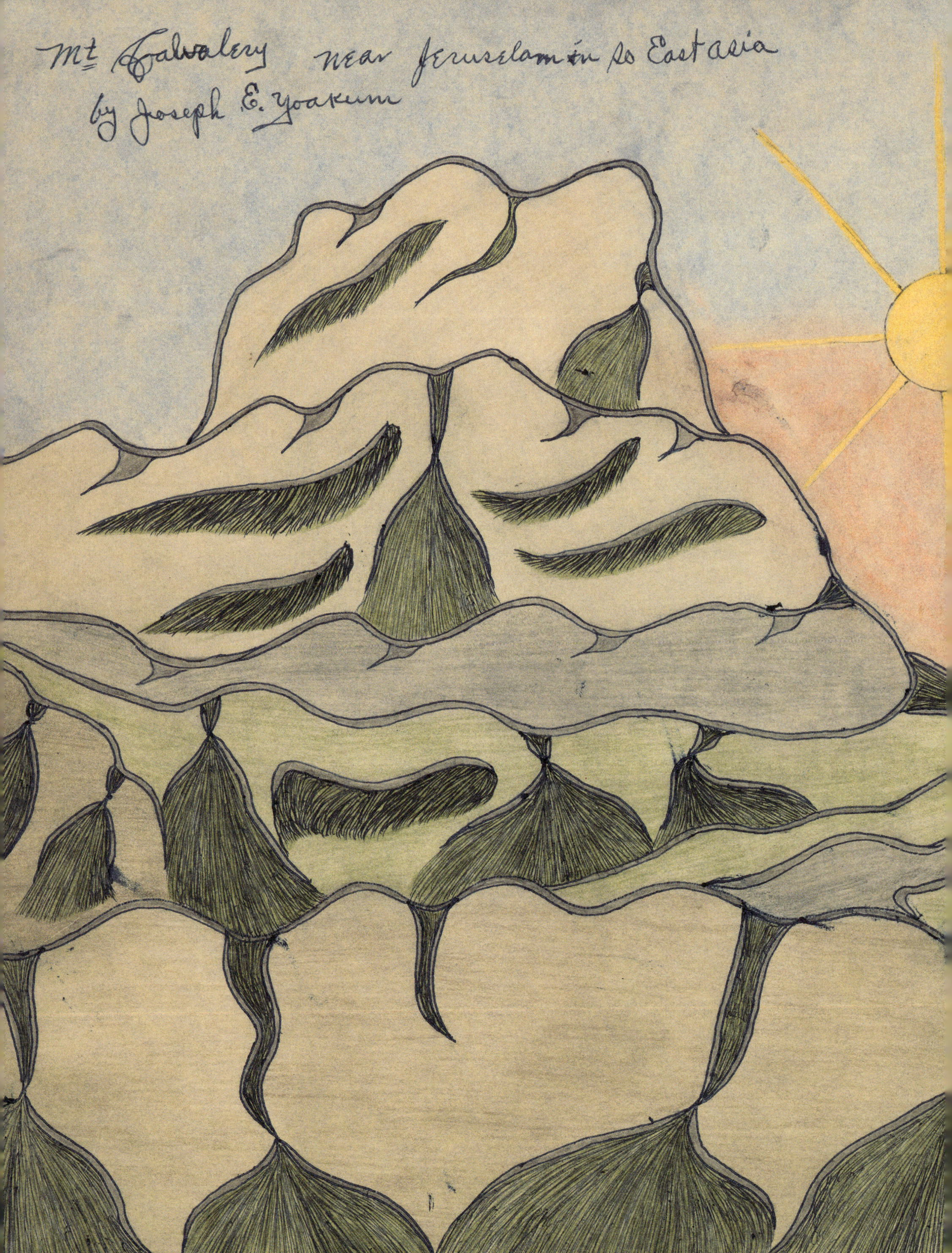
Mt Calvalery near Jeruselam in So East asia
by Joseph E. Yoakum

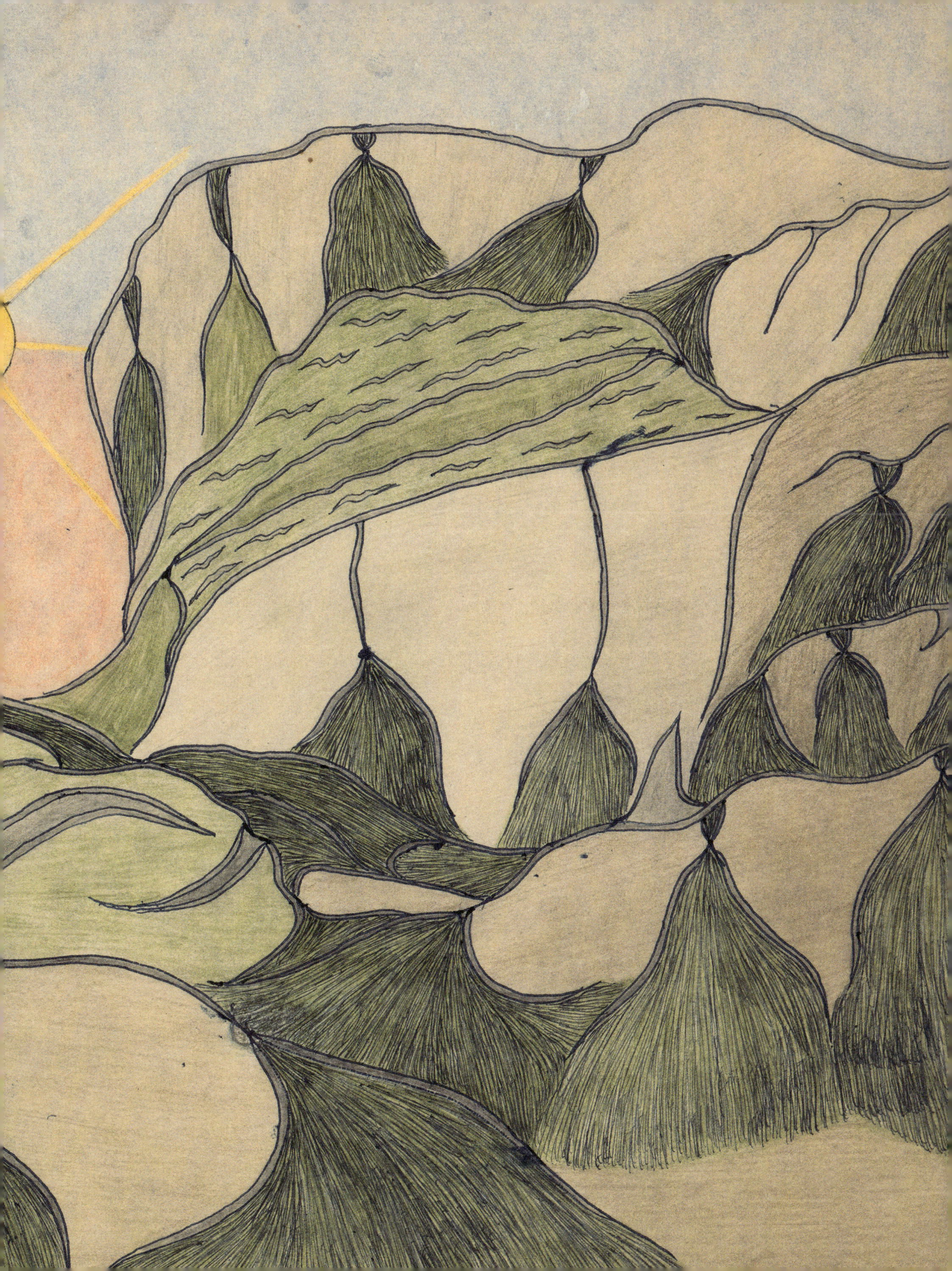

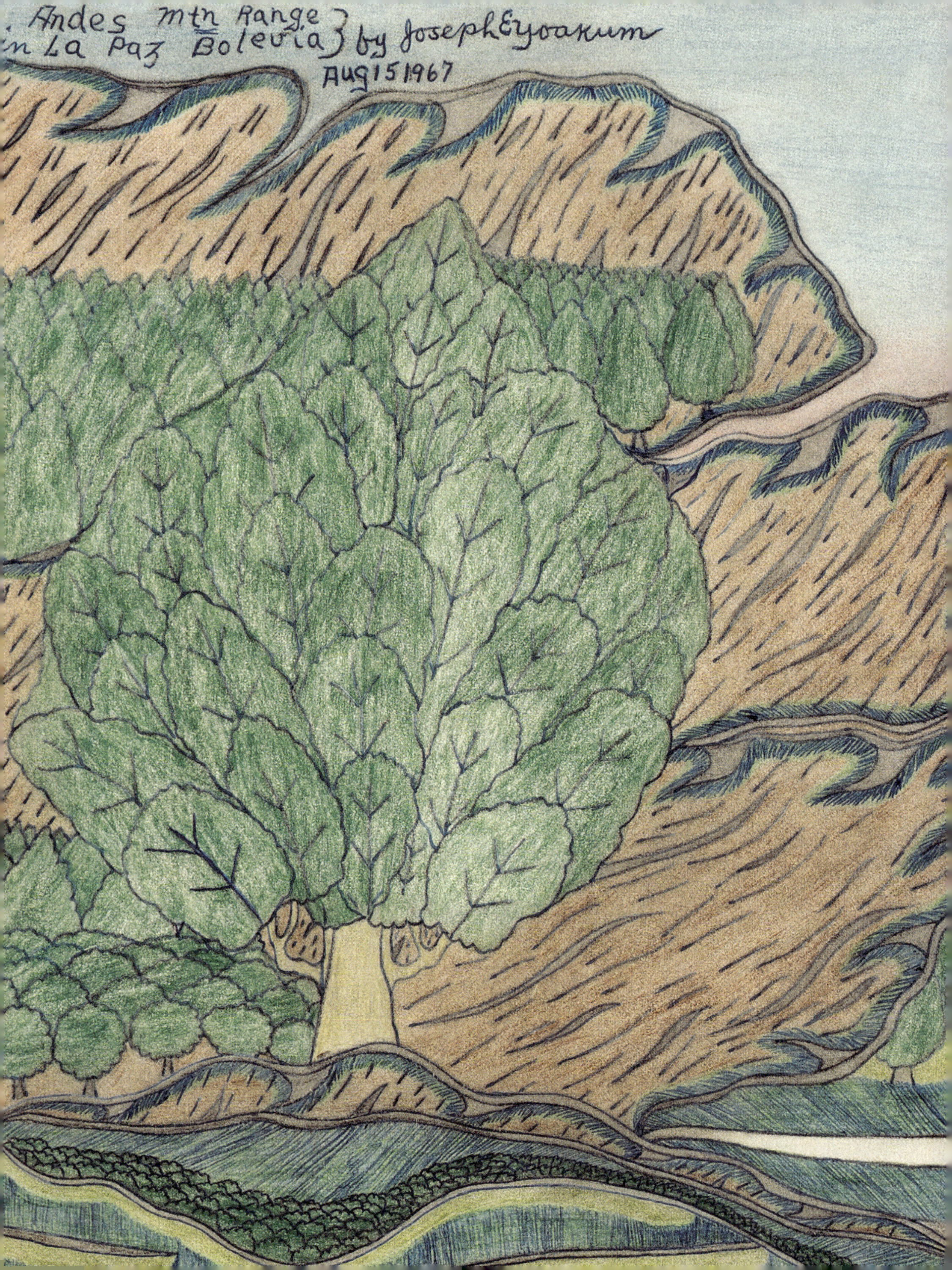
Andes mtn Range
in La Paz Bolevia
by JosephEYoakum
Aug151967

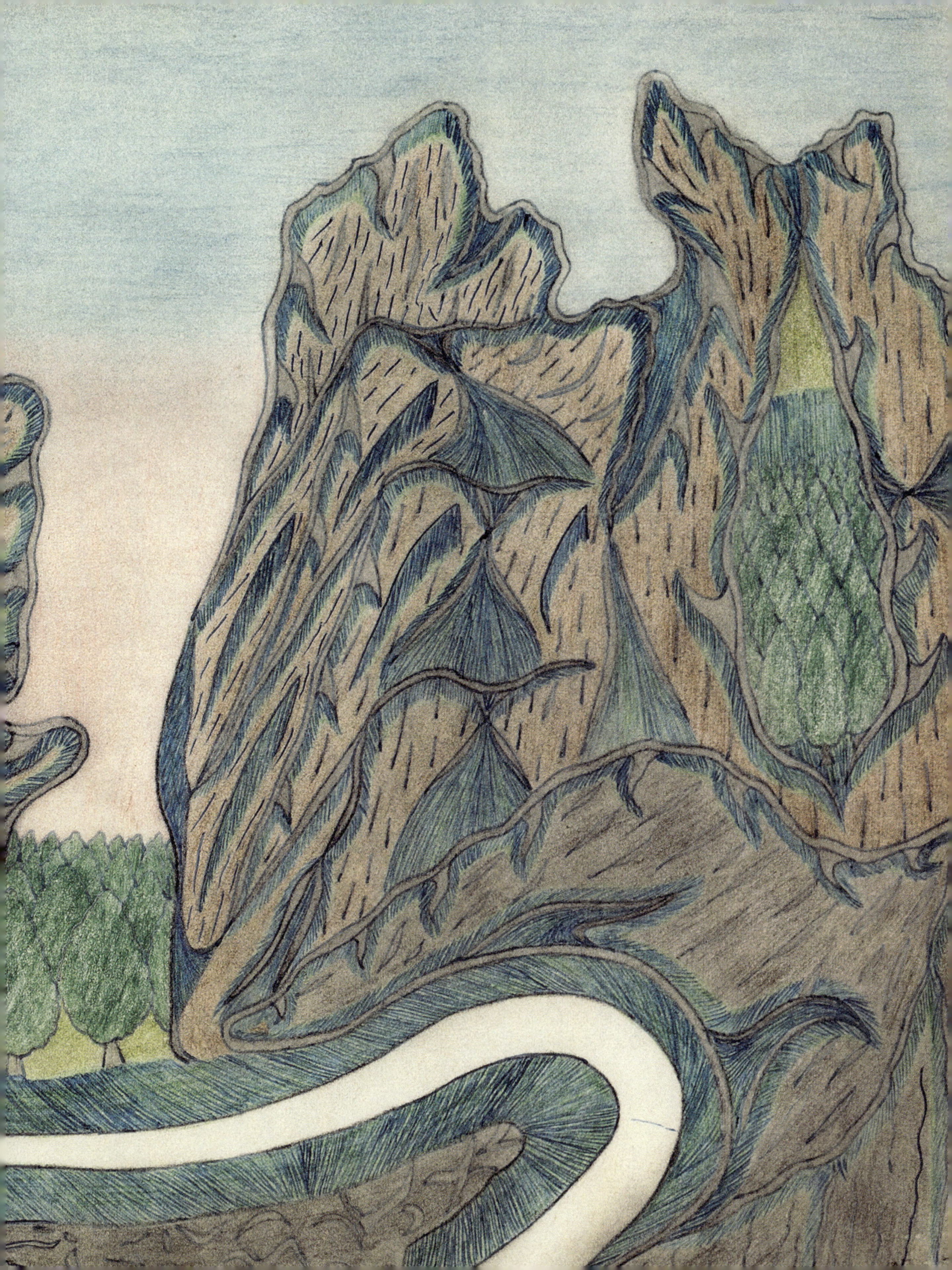

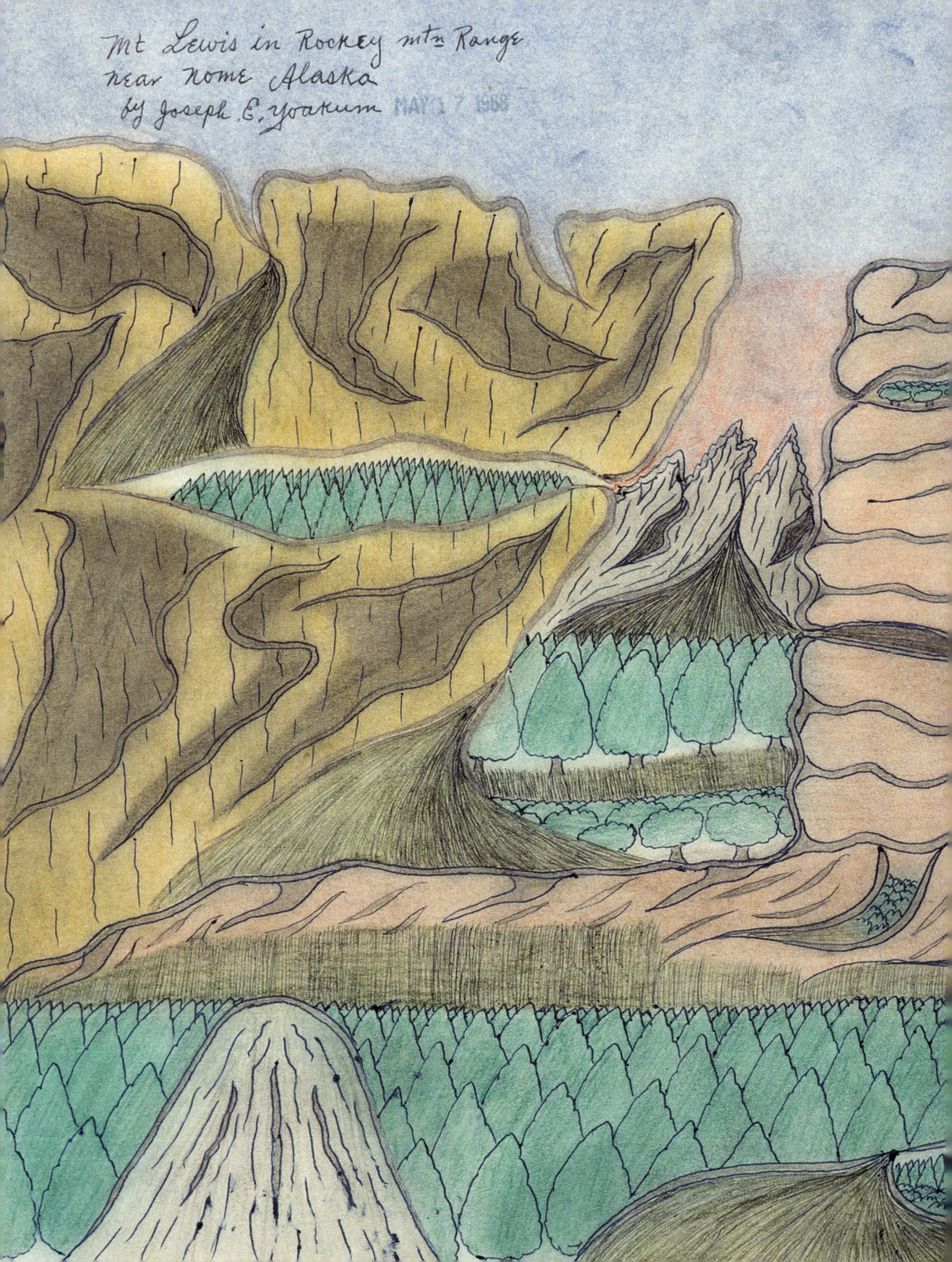
Mt Lewis in Rockey mtn Range
near Nome Alaska
by Joseph E. Yoakum
MAY 17 1968

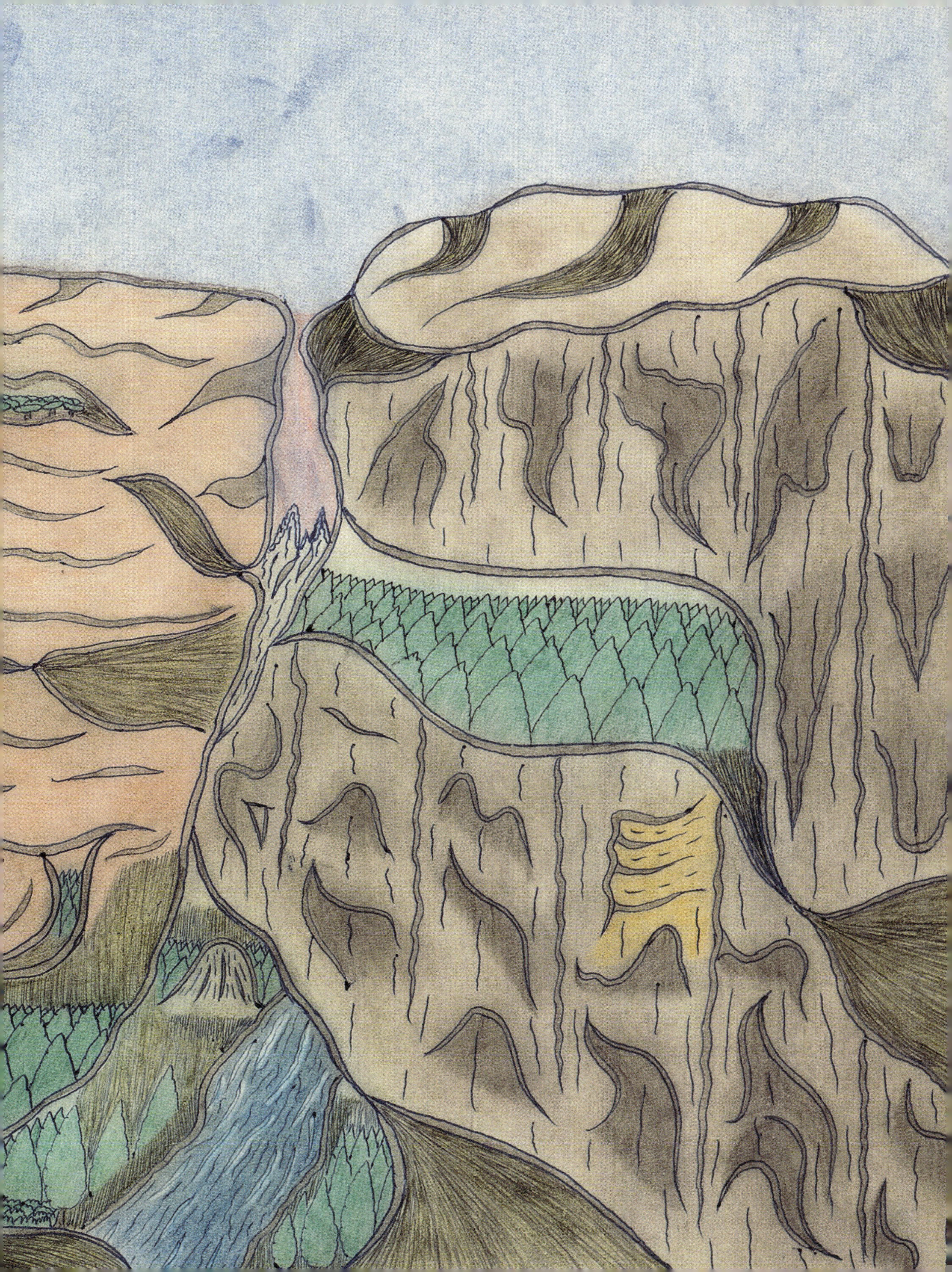

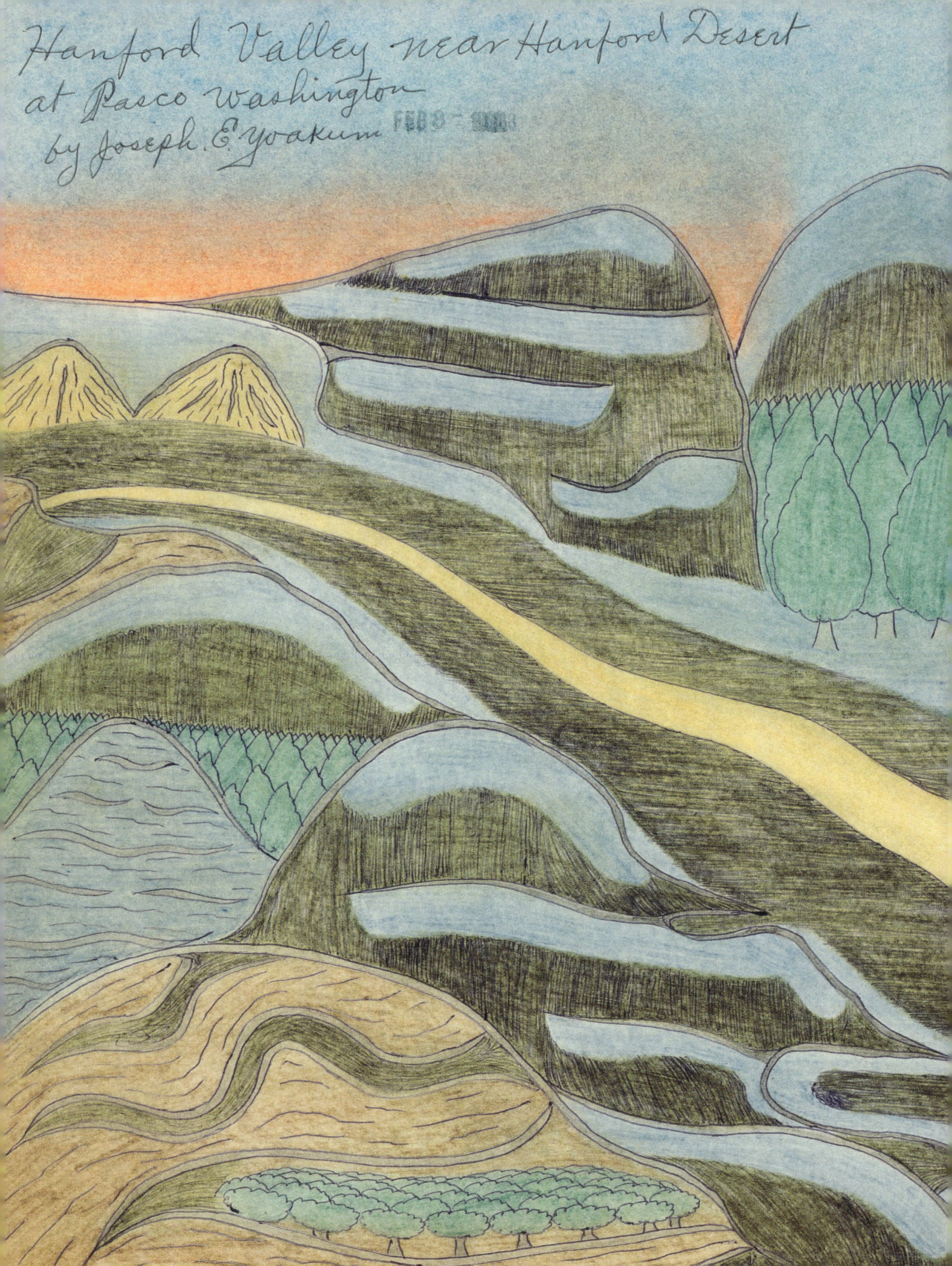
Hanford Valley near Hanford Desert
at Pasco Washington
by Joseph. E. Yoakum

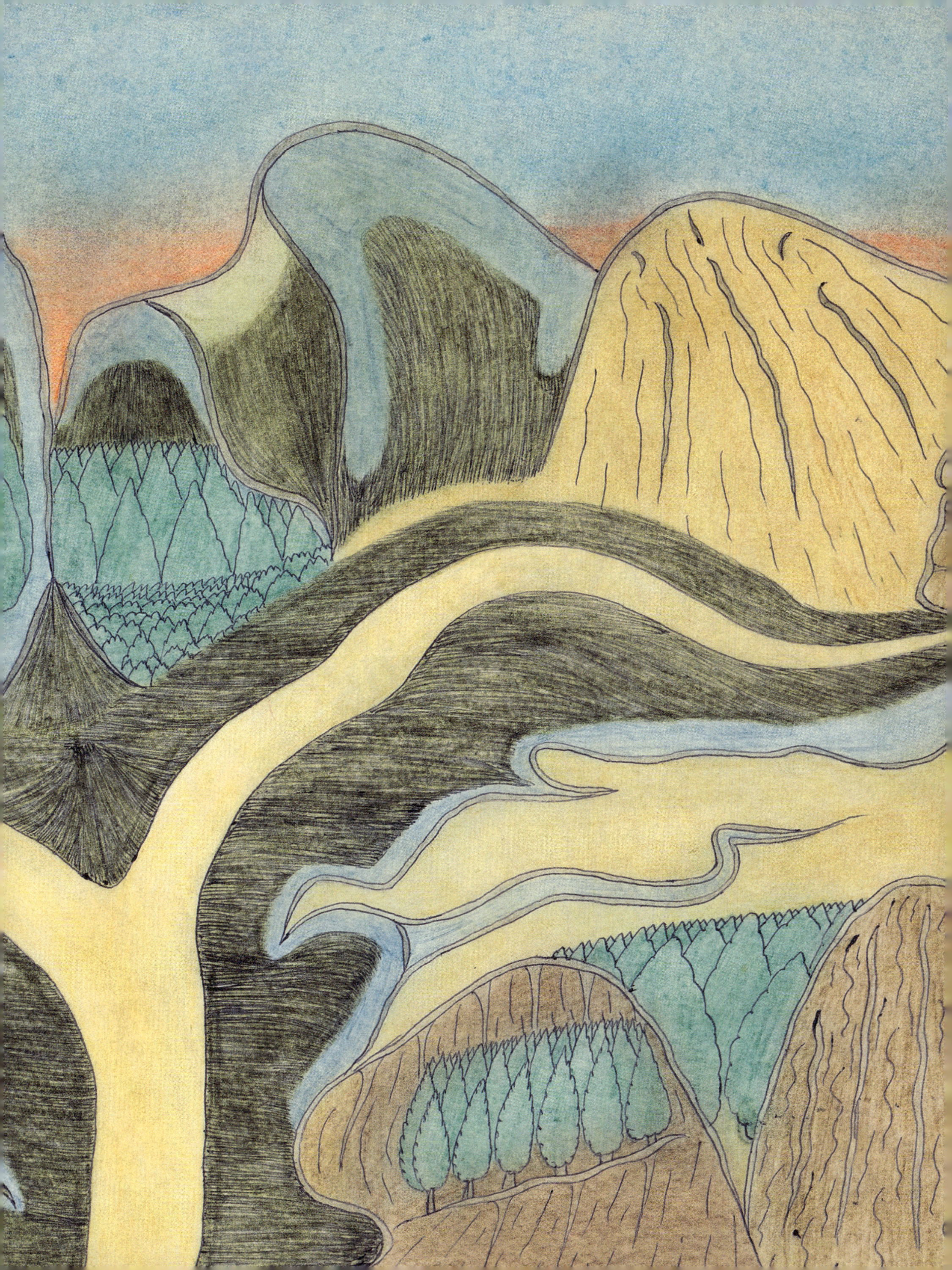

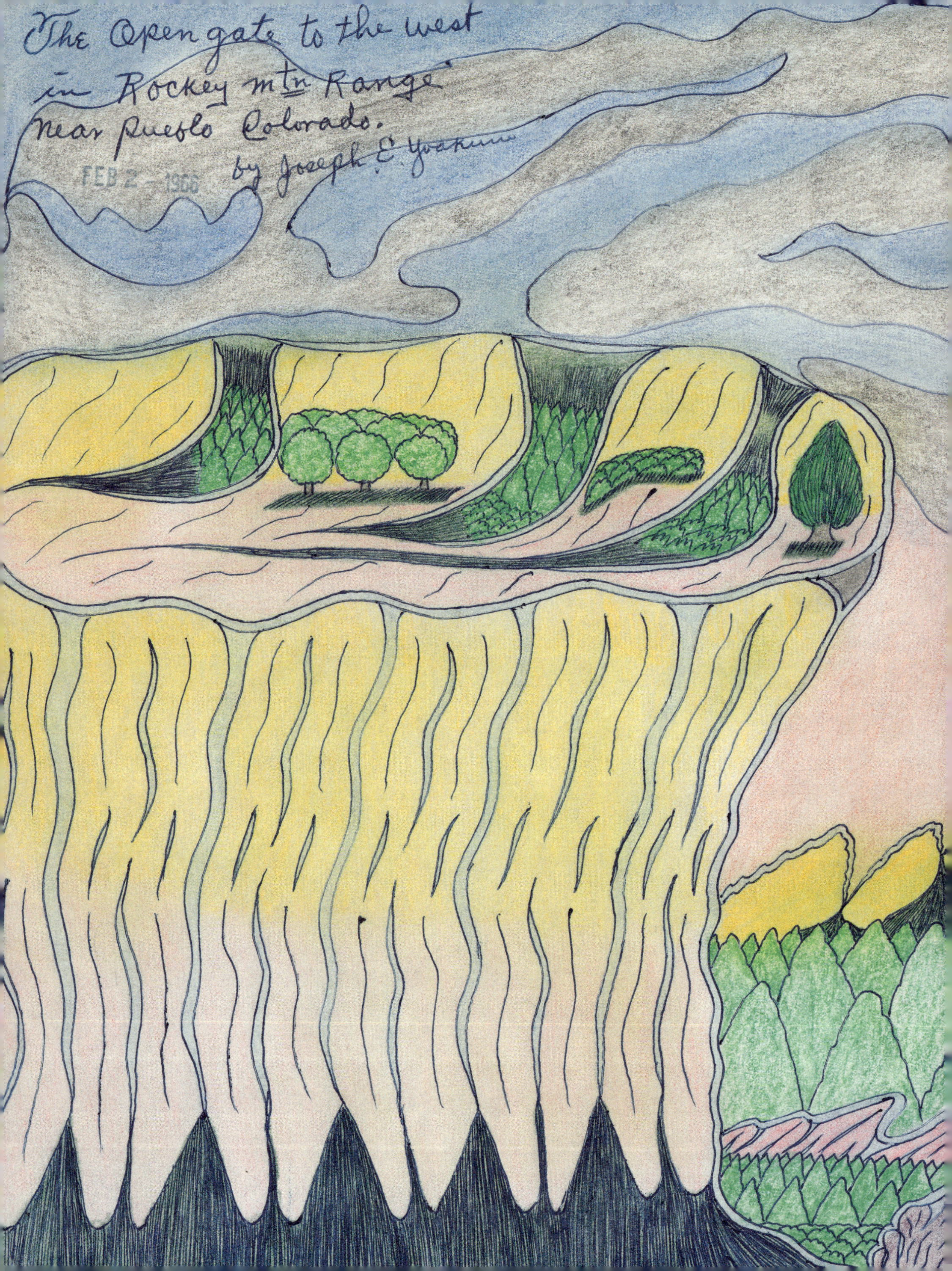

The Open gate to the west
in Rockey mtn Range
near pueblo Colorado.
by Joseph E. Yoakum

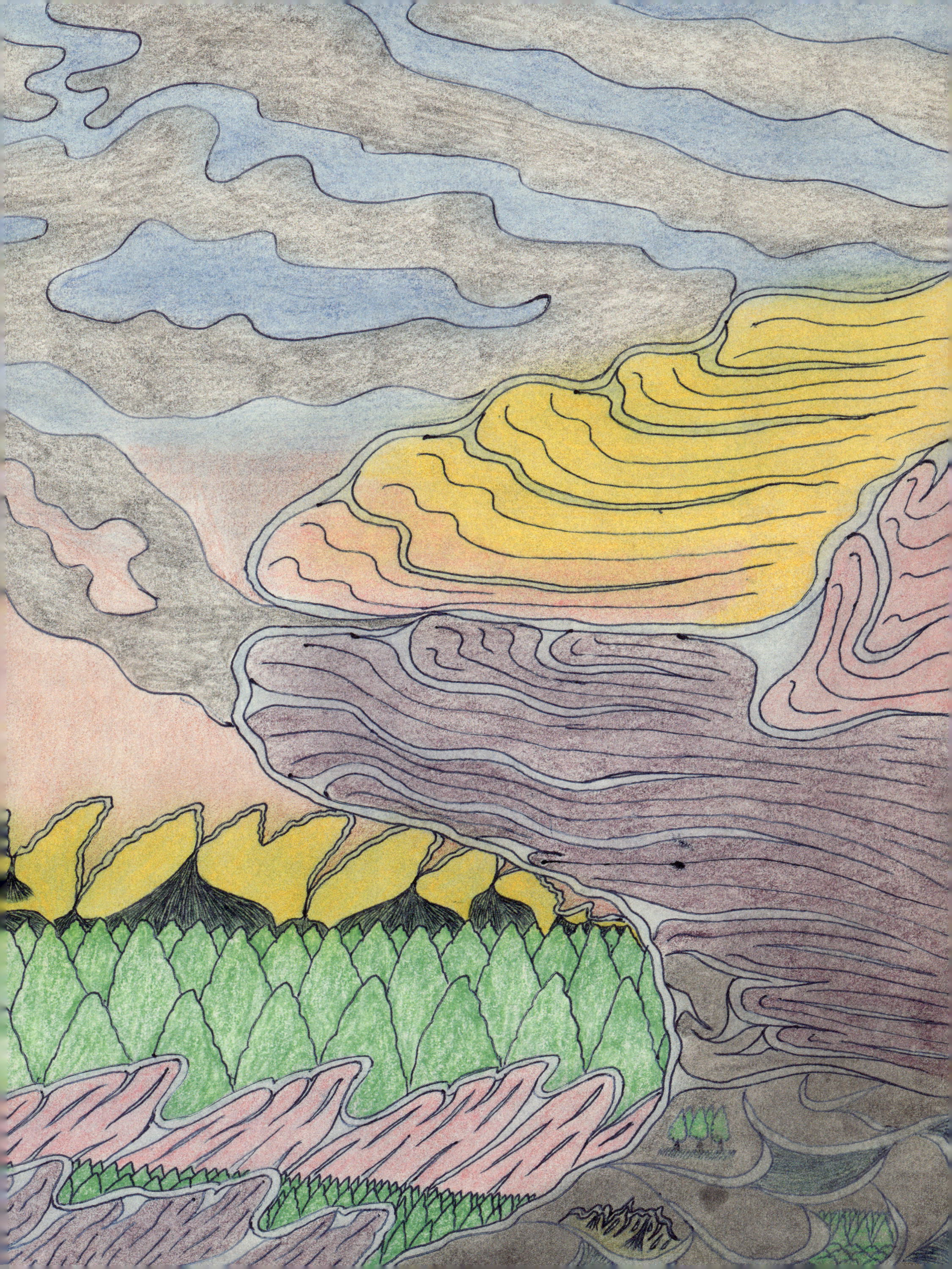

Granit Center Mound in Rockey Range
near Nome Alaska
by Joseph E. Yoakum

FEB. 27 1970

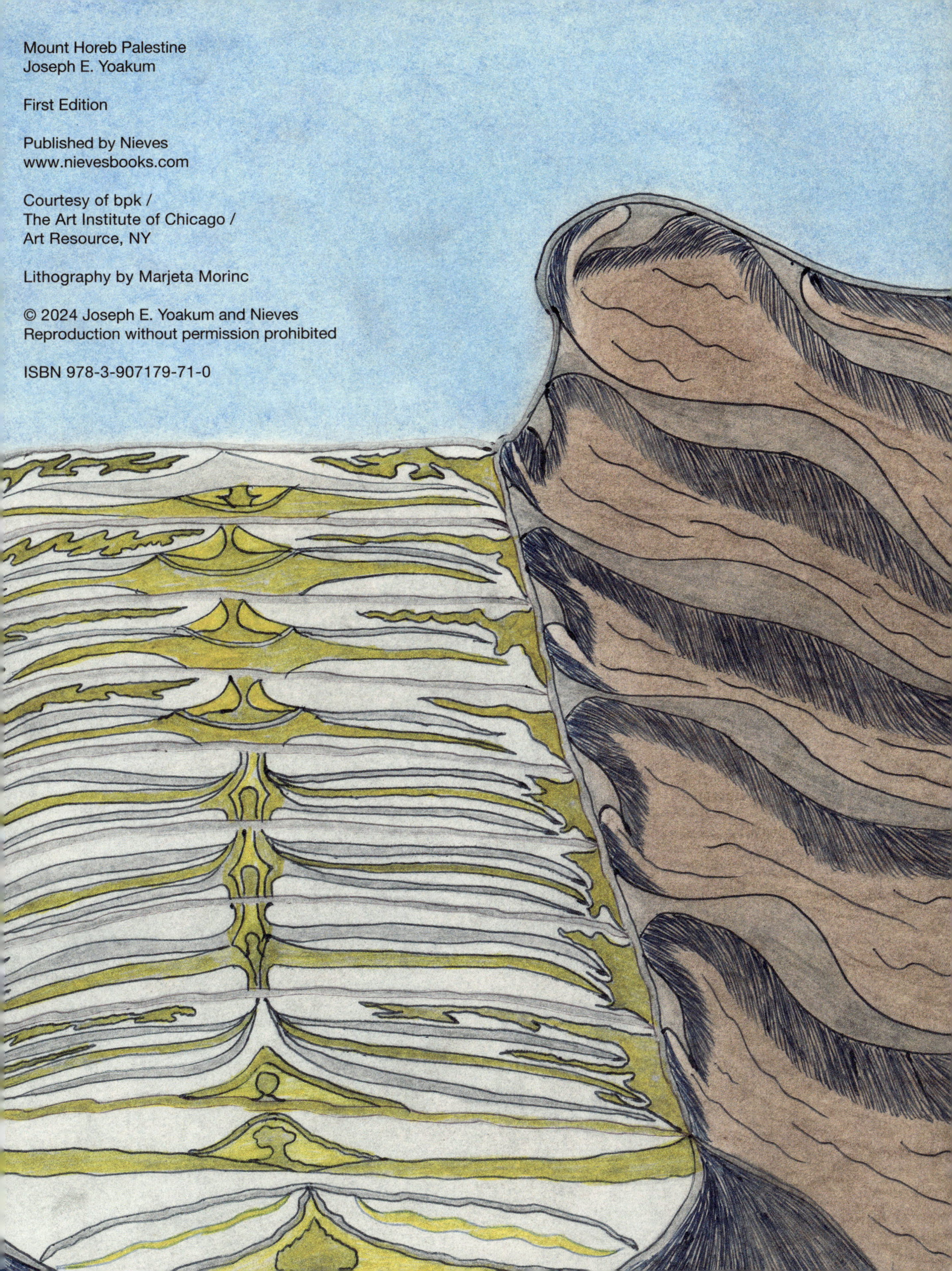

Mount Horeb Palestine
Joseph E. Yoakum

First Edition

Published by Nieves
www.nievesbooks.com

Courtesy of bpk /
The Art Institute of Chicago /
Art Resource, NY

Lithography by Marjeta Morinc

ISBN 978-3-907179-71-0

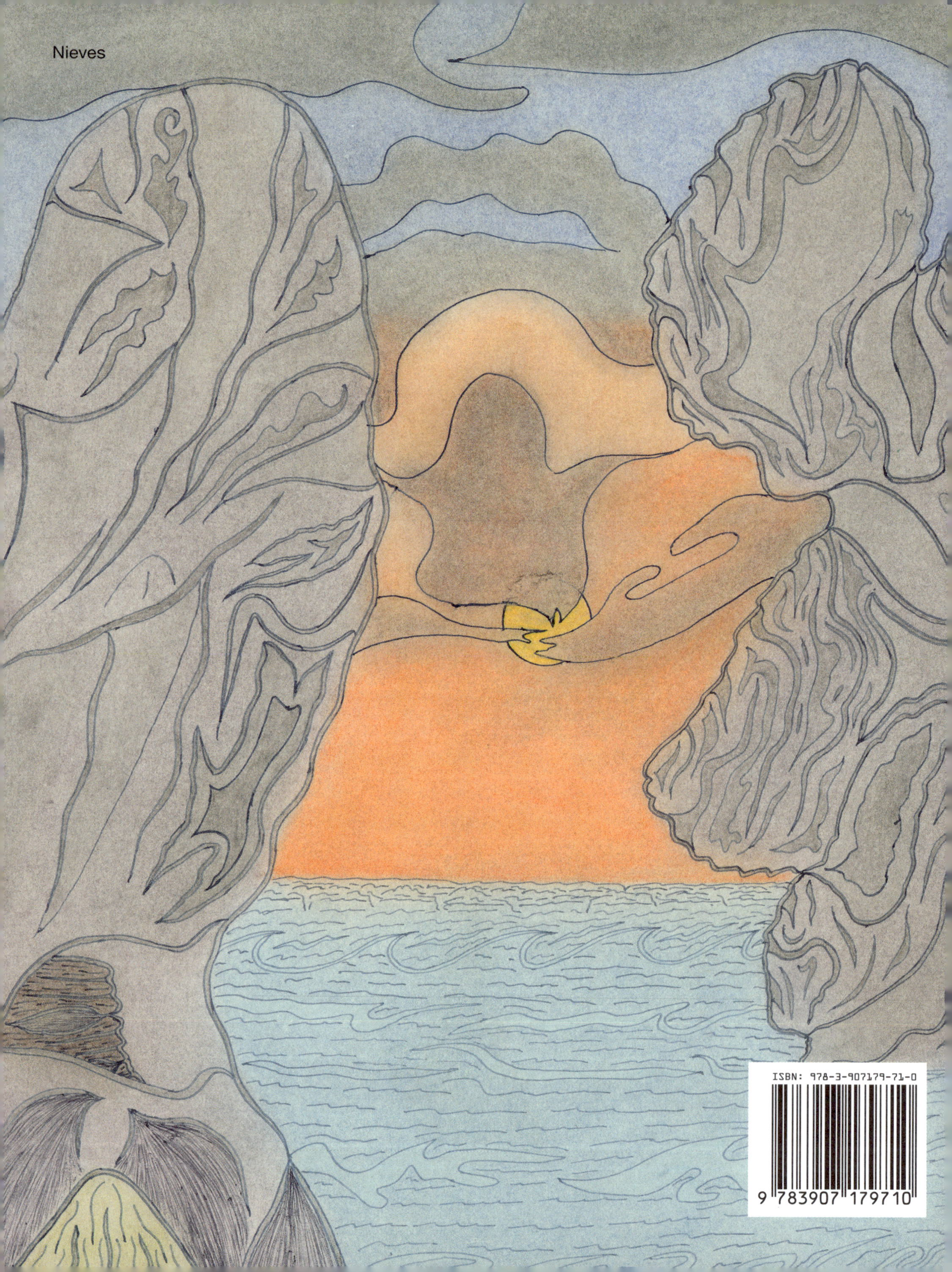

ISBN: 978-3-907179-71-0
9 783907 179710